NAMIBIA
‹THE BEAUTIFUL LAND›

NAMIBIA

‹THE BEAUTIFUL LAND›

Text by David Bristow

STRUIK

Struik Publishers (a member of The Struik Group (Pty) Ltd)
Cornelis Struik House
80 McKenzie Street
Cape Town
8001
Reg. No.: 63/00203/07

First published 1990
Second impression 1992

Text © David Bristow

PHOTOGRAPHIC CREDITS

Mark van Aardt: pages 6/7, 10/11, 16 (top & bottom), 17 (top), 18 (top & bottom)
19 (top), 20 (centre & bottom), 21 (top & centre), 24, 26 (top & bottom), 28, 29, 36/37,
38, 43, 44, 46 (top), 47, 48, 49 (top), 52 (bottom), 55 (bottom), 60 (top), 62, 78, 79,
(top & bottom)
Peter Pickford: pages 1, 2/3, 5, 20 (top), 21 (bottom), 25 (top & bottom),
39, 40/41, 49 (bottom), 50/51, 52 (top), 53, 56/57, 58, 60 (bottom), 61, 63 (bottom),
64, 65 (top & bottom), 66, 67, 68, 69, 70, 71, 72/73, 74, 75, 76/77, 80
Walter Knirr: pages 8/9, 12/13, 22/23, 31, 32/33, 35, 42, 54, 55 (top)
Gerald Cubitt: cover, pages 30, 34, 46 (bottom)
Keith Young: pages 17 (bottom), 59
Anglo American Corporation of South Africa Limited: page 19 (centre & bottom)
David Bristow: page 18 (centre)
Hu Berry: page 63 (top)

Layout by Joan Sutton Design Studio c.c.
Typesetting by Hirt & Carter (Pty) Ltd, Cape Town
Reproduction by Unifoto (Pty) Ltd, Cape Town
Printed and bound by Kyodo Printing Co (Singapore) Pte Ltd

ISBN 1 86825 070 9

FRONTISPIECE *The yellow mongoose is found throughout Namibia, in all but the most severe desert areas.*

PREVIOUS PAGE *Giraffes are, for obvious reasons, among the most conspicuous animals on the uniformly flat plains of the Etosha National Park.*

OPPOSITE *The male lion – commonly named the 'king of beasts' – is, in fact, a lazy animal, who prefers to leave hunting to the females. When he does decide to hunt, however, he will provide an awesome display of power and aggression.*

OVERLEAF *Although the highly mineralized waters at Ai-Ais are not fit for human consumption, they are reputed to have health-giving properties when bathed in. The water emerges from the ground at 66 °C, and is cooled in pools to a bearable temperature.*

PAGES 8+9 *The gemsbok, or oryx, is Namibia's national animal, and depicted on its current coat of arms. While forthcoming events in the territory are likely to see a change in its political emblems, the gemsbok will remain a symbol of the country's vast, arid conservation areas.*

PAGES 10+11 *In Africa, even the most delicate flush of nature is likely to conceal a barb. The yellow flowers that spring up after the infrequent rains grow from the same plant that spreads vicious, three-spiked thorns across the countryside.*

PAGES 12+13 *Between the Namib sand-sea, which hugs the coastline, and the mountains of the slightly less arid Pro-Namib area, gravel plains stretch across the bleak terrain. It looks rugged and uncompromising, but the ecosystem here is extremely sensitive to disturbance. Fortunately, most of the desert falls within conservation areas. Recreational facilities are mostly basic, such as the popular camp site at Sesriem, seen here.*

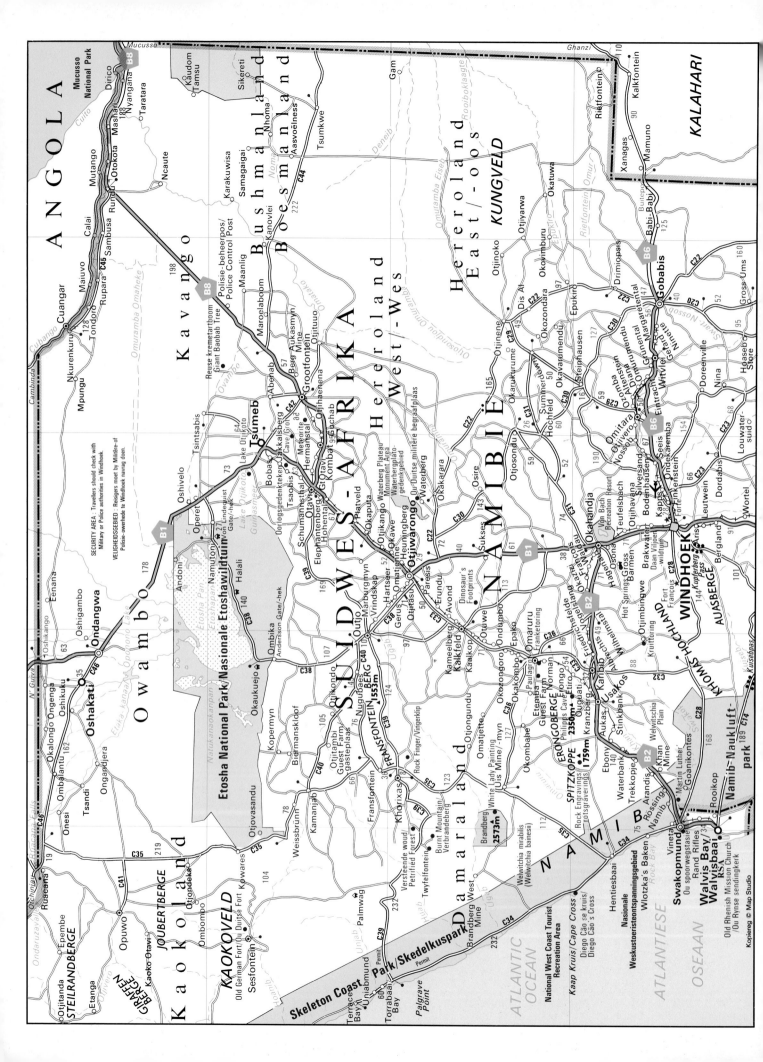

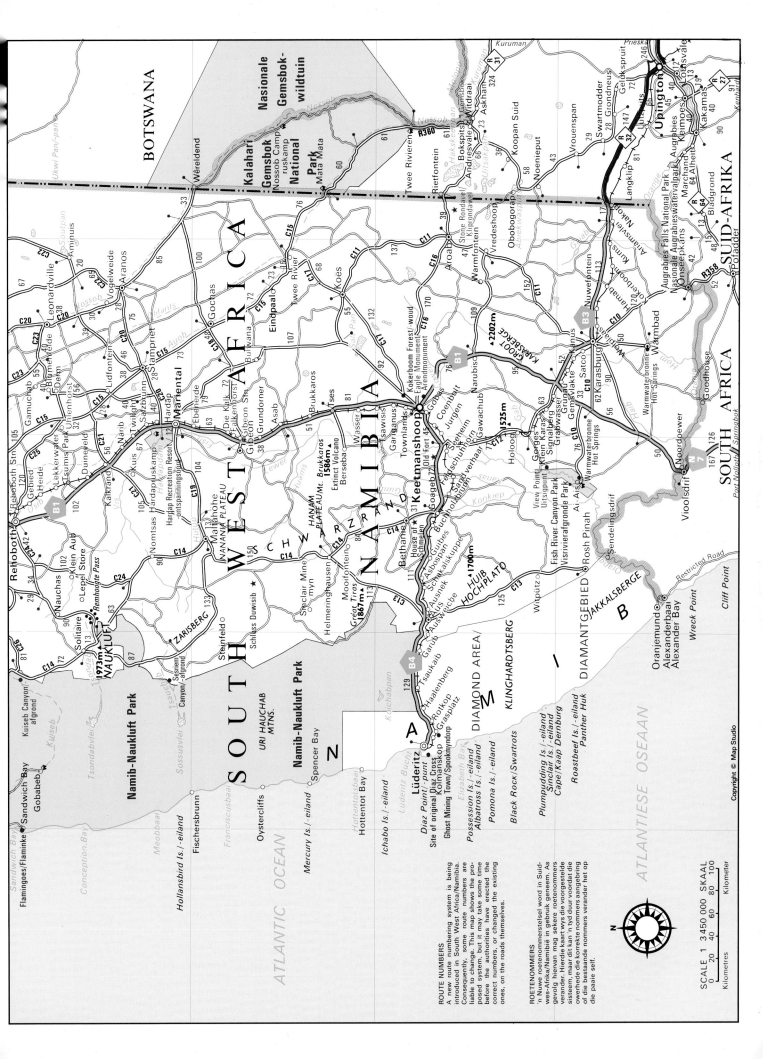

INTRODUCTION

*N*AMIBIA IS A HUGE COUNTRY, more in the sense of its grandeur than in its actual geographical area, although at over 800 000 square kilometres it is hardly small. It is a country with seemingly nothing but huge open spaces dominated by surreal landscapes. With the exception of the Caprivi Strip's wetlands and lakes in the extreme northeast, Namibia is a thirstland; its rivers are more likely to flow with sand than with water. For the people that live in these arid regions, theirs is an arduous existence, but for the well-prepared visitor, it is a place of spectacular beauty and grandeur. Even in the harshest of environments, there is a surprising quantity of large game, as well as smaller animals and bizarre plants adapted to the punishing conditions. Look at a map – the exotic, tongue-tangling names let you know immediately that you are entering 'terra incognito' – adventure lies before you.

The physical landscape of Namibia comprises three main components: the coastal plain, the Great Escarpment, and the interior plateau. The entire coastal plain is a desert and semi-desert expanse, averaging about 100 kilometres in width – a universe of sand and sky. At the edge of this region is a chain of mountains and topographical steps that forms a barrier between it and the interior plateau of arid, but comparatively fertile, grasslands. This is ranching and game country, dominated by flat-topped umbrella thorn trees and tall, column-like termitaria.

Roughly in the centre of the country lies its capital city, Windhoek, with a population of a little over 100 000. In spite of its small size, Windhoek has something of a cosmopolitan air about it. Here, nineteenth century German architecture co-exists with twentieth century office blocks, and the vibrant colours of the Herero women's dress mingle with the more sombre attire of Windhoek businessmen.

Almost 300 kilometres to the west of Windhoek lies Swakopmund. This small town seems to have been gently picked up from the Bavarian countryside by some fantastical hand and, as a joke, deposited on Namibia's bleak coast. The road between Windhoek and Swakopmund, the two most popular tourist towns, conveniently divides the country into two manageable sections. The principal attraction of southern Namibia is the Namib Desert, most of which is protected within the Namib-Naukluft Park. South of the park lies the forbidden diamond area, or *Sperrgebiet*, which continues down to the Orange River; to the north the Skeleton Coast Park stretches up to the Angolan border. The country's entire coastline is, therefore, protected against human intrusion, making it unequalled in the world of conservation.

The Namib is the world's oldest and driest desert, its annual rainfall of less than 25 millimetres falling mostly in short cloudbursts. Some places may not feel the life-giving, cool caress of rain for decades at a time, but when it does rain, a sudden growth of silver grasses softens the rugged countryside like a dusting of cosmetic powder on a wrinkled, sun-cracked skin. Scant as the vegetation is, it supports a surprising variety of animal life, from tiny ants and beetles to large mammals – zebra, gemsbok and springbok, and their predators.

The arid climate is determined by the cold Benguela Current that courses up the continent's west coast. For millions of years, a stream of nutrient-rich, polar-chilled water from the Antarctic has surged along the Atlantic floor. When it reaches the African continental shelf, it is forced to the surface. The consequent cold surface-temperature of the sea here inhibits the formation of rain clouds, so cool coastal winds bear no rain to ease the land's thirst. But, where the air-masses from the icy sea and burning land meet, the atmospheric moisture condenses to form dense fog banks, which the sea breezes carry up to 50 kilometres inland, across the dunes and gravel plains.

Most visitors use Swakopmund as a base for explorations into the desert. From here, one can take a day's trip along the Namib Welwitschia Nature Drive, criss-crossing the dry Swakop River bed and its rugged flanking hills. After passing the other-worldly 'moonscape' formed by the Swakop River valley, the route enters a wide gravel plain, and here, on this forsaken, wind-scoured expanse where nothing other than crusty lichens should exist, the crumpled forms of welwitschia plants (*Welwitschia mirabilis*) stud the ground – a living link between cone-bearing and flowering plants. Large specimens, standing up to 1,5 metres high, are well over 1 000 years old, and the oldest nearly double that.

Another worthwhile day trip from Swakopmund is to Sandwich Harbour, a bird paradise that lies among the nearby coastal dunes. This unique coastal lagoon, part tidal and part freshwater, is formed where the Kuiseb River's underground flow seeps onto the beach to create a haven for flamingoes, pelicans, terns, avocets, herons and ducks.

The Kuiseb is one of the major watercourses cutting across the Namib Desert, dividing it into gravel plains to the north and a 'sand sea' to the south. Although it is dry for most of its course, there is a continual subterranean flow that allows large trees to flourish in the shady gorge, and pools persist on the stream bed in all but the driest years.

The river flows only once or twice every decade, seldom reaching the coast at Walvis Bay. The last time it did reach the sea was over 50 years ago, and there is little doubt that it will find its way there again, at some time in the future. Until then, however, man's short-term memory allows him to build a town right on the Kuiseb's sandy delta, in the mouth of Walvis Bay.

About 100 kilometres south of the Kuiseb, at Sossusvlei, are the world's highest sand dunes, whose crests twist like the bodies of writhing serpents. In this wide crescent of interlocking dunes the Tsauchab River is trapped, its infrequent waters quickly sucked up by the sun to leave a salt-bleached pan floor.

Because of its great age, the Namib has an extraordinary number of creatures adapted to this harshest of environments – none more so than its beetles. Many beetles and other small creatures of the 'sand sea' area, such as moles and mice, lizards and snakes, literally swim through the dunes. With surface temperatures reaching up to 70 °C at midday, and falling to below freezing at night, these creatures are able to maintain a constant body temperature by moving up or down within the sand mass.

Just over 200 kilometres south of Sossusvlei lies Lüderitz, the almost-forgotten town that was the first permanent European settlement to be established in Namibia. The road to Lüderitz from Keetmanshoop traverses a forsaken stretch of land; an eerie and vacant expanse along which ox wagons once hauled water to the desert-besieged port that is truly at the end of the line. Just inland of Lüderitz, the diamond boom settlement of Kolmanskop, now a ghost town, reclines on a deep mantle of sand. The town sprang up on a rich pocket of alluvial diamonds in the most inhospitable part of the Namib, but as soon as the diamonds were exhausted, it was abandoned. Now the ever-marching dunes advance across the streets and invade the buildings, reclaiming them for the desert.

The country's southernmost attraction is the Fish River Canyon, second only to Colorado's Grand Canyon as the world's most spectacular river-forged formation. From a viewpoint at the canyon's northern end, a hiking trail winds its way down through tiered bands of sandstone, shale and limestone, to reach the river bed after one vertical kilometre. From here, it is a three-day trek to the mineral spa resort of Ai-Ais which lies at the southern end of the main canyon.

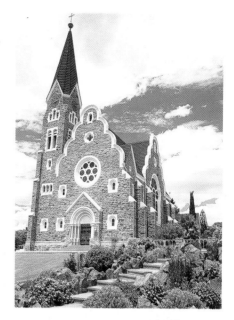

TOP *German Rhenish missionaries were among the first Europeans to settle north of the Orange River. They established mission stations throughout the country, from which to spread their word. Many of the Lutheran churches in Namibia originated from their teachings, an impressive example of which is this one overlooking Windhoek.*
ABOVE *The various Herero tribes take great pride in self-adornment. The women of the major Herero group – from the country's central region – adapted their style of dress from the Victorian fashions worn by early missionaries' wives.*

'Land of Contrasts' is an often-used phrase to describe Namibia; this is most true of the country's northern section, which grades from the arid Namib Desert to the riverine forests of the Caprivi wetlands. Starting from the wreck-littered Skeleton Coast, we move inland across the searing gravel plains of the desert and into the gnarled, burnished mountains of the Kaokoveld. Beyond these the land levels out on the sand flats and floodplains of Ovamboland. When explorer Charles Andersson travelled through this area a century ago, it was covered by dense mopane forest and palm-fringed pans. Today, after heavy overgrazing and the cutting of timber, it more closely resembles the surrounding desert than the 'oasis' that Andersson described.

Between here and Windhoek lies Damaraland, which comprises desert, semi-desert and arid savanna. In the semi-desert area lying between the Namib and the farming lands, small herds of black rhino and elephant cling to their shrivelling territories. The country's highest mountain outcrops occur here – the Erongos and Spitzkoppe, and the Brandberg range which, after the Drakensberg and Maluti ranges of Lesotho and central South Africa, is the highest in southern Africa. On a biological interface between Damaraland and Ovamboland, the Etosha National Park, pride of the country's game reserves, is Namibia's single most popular tourist attraction.

There are few places left in Africa where game can be seen in such abundance as at Etosha – vast herds of springbok and zebra, multitudes of gemsbok and giraffe, a large lion population, elephant herds, and black rhino all abound here. The lilacbreasted rollers, kori bustards and korhaans, eagles and ostriches, bush shrikes, egrets, herons and flamingoes would amaze even the most casual observer of bird life. In the dry season, the game congregates around the water holes to make viewing easy, while in the wet season the park is closed, as the risk of contracting malaria is extremely high and, in wet years, the area becomes completely inundated. When this happens, the great salt pan becomes the most important breeding site in southern Africa for the lesser and greater flamingoes – a phenomenon which, unfortunately, is rarely seen by visitors.

The shallow, tepid waters do not last for long in this dry climate, and as they vanish they leave behind a smooth, white skin of salt, like an animal hide stretched tautly over an African drum. In the heat of midday, the sun beats down on this surface, the booming silence broken only by the shrill ring of cicada beetles. Mirages vibrate on the pan's bleached surface, from which comes the name 'Etosha', variously translated as the 'place of mirages' or 'place of dry water'. However, the images of gemsbok and ostrich, which seem to melt in the liquid panorama, are real enough.

Namutoni, Etosha's northernmost rest-camp, began its life as a German fort during the colonial wars against the Ovambo people at the turn of the century. The fort was built next to one of the few artesian springs in this hostile area. In 1904, it was attacked by a strong Ovambo force, who plundered it before burning it down.

TOP *Woermann House was built in Swakopmund in 1894, and is preserved as an excellent example of the German colonial architecture of the period. Swakopmund itself, where Germanic styles and customs still predominate, is Namibia's most attractive town.*
CENTRE *The short-lived boom town of Kolmanskop slowly recedes into the desert sands that gave it life. It was here, in 1908, that the country's first diamonds were discovered, but after* only two decades, the supply of gems was exhausted, and the once-bustling town was soon deserted.
BOTTOM *Lüderitz, the first European town in 'South West Africa', was established by German traders, and from here their colony expanded. After numerous booms and collapses, this isolated harbour town languishes in the economic doldrums, with tourism offering the only breeze of hope.*

Namutoni was soon recaptured by a stronger German force, and rebuilt in its present form. Today, the crenellated fort serves as a headquarters for man's fight against poachers, who, driven by the promise of riches, turn automatic rifles against the country's small remaining elephant and rhino populations.

Travelling to the northeast from Etosha, we cross the monotonously flat Kavango region; only one muddy or sandy track, depending on the season, leads for 500 kilometres towards the Caprivi Strip, an area that resembles Botswana's Okavango Delta and is, in fact, part of the same drainage system. The Caprivi Strip is not on the general tourist route, as access to it is limited and there are no tourist facilities. Like the Kaokoveld, however, it is a place of rare adventure, where the well-prepared traveller can still experience the African wilderness in its primordial state.

It is the very inhospitability of Namibia's wild regions that has allowed them to remain unspoilt for so long. The harshness of the country's desert and the inaccessibility of its wetlands do not entice those looking for the easy life. The first white man known to have set foot on Namibian sand was the Portuguese navigator, Diego Cão, who in 1485 erected a padrão (stone cross) at what is now called Cape Cross. Cão's voyage was one of several Portuguese 'voyages of discovery' – attempts to find a sea-route to the East once Turkish domination of the Middle East had sealed off trade routes between Europe and Asia.

But, as was the case throughout southern Africa, the first people known to live here were bands of San hunter-gatherers. For thousands of years they lived off the land, following the herds of game, which in turn followed the intermittent rains across the subcontinent. Because their numbers were always low, the San were easily pushed aside when Negroid herders and cultivators – Ovambos and Kavangos – drifted down from Central Africa before the arrival of white people in the area.

While their numbers were low and fertile land was plentiful, everyone lived easy, pastoral lives. A later wave of migrants, from the lakes of Central Africa, were the Herero people. They moved west until they came across the unoccupied but barren Kaokoveld badlands and, for a while, settled there. Towards the middle of the eighteenth century, the main body of Hereros moved southeastward, to the fertile grazing lands of the interior plateau. Poorer offshoots, the Himba and Tjimba, were left in the Kaokoveld's wastelands, and there they remain, tenuously, as curious and fascinating cultures which open a door on man's past.

In the early 1800s, a clan of the Nama people, escaping Dutch dominance at the Cape far to the south, settled at a strong perennial spring in the centre of what is now Namibia. Their leader, Jonker Afrikaner, named the place after the Winterhoek Mountains, his birthplace in the Cape. Because of its central location, reliable spring and pleasant surroundings, this settlement soon became a major trading centre. By then, white hunters and traders had established a steady trade in ivory and skins, dried meat, ostrich feathers

TOP *Diamonds are still recovered in vast quantities from Namibia's diamond coast or* Sperrgebiet. *In our nuclear age, however, the country's rich uranium deposits are fast becoming its most important mineral asset. These uranium crystals come from the open-cast mine at Rössing, near Swakopmund.*

CENTRE *One week's production of diamonds at Consolidated Diamond Mines (CDM).*

BOTTOM *An Ovambo miner at CDM. This diamond-mining operation is one of Namibia's top employers of skilled and semi-skilled personnel. Here, in a highly sophisticated operation, some 70 million tons of sand are moved each year to reach the diamonds that lie on the bedrock up to 14 metres below sea-level.*

and cattle, mainly in return for guns and alcohol. Today, Afrikaner's resting place is known as Windhoek, and is the country's capital and only city. In an essentially arid land, it was a coveted place, and, with pressure for land building up from north and south, conflict was inevitable.

From about 1840 onwards, the various Nama and Herero tribes became embroiled in a series of vicious wars whose excesses of cruelty and vengeance knew no limits. These feuds lasted for over 50 years, drawing in early white traders, then missionaries, and later German troops when the territory became a colony in 1884.

Until this time few Europeans had ventured to settle in this forbidding land. A century before, American and British whaling fleets had been using the natural harbours at Walvis Bay and nearby Sandwich Harbour during their whaling and sealing activities in these resource-rich southern waters. In 1793, the Dutch at the Cape annexed all the principal bays along the southwest African coast in an attempt to forestall foreign occupation. When the British took control of the Cape Colony two years later, they hoisted the Union Jack at these ports. This was primarily to limit whaling to British ships, for the land itself seemed to offer them little, other than sandstorms, thirst and heat.

Among the first Europeans to cross the Orange River from the Cape Colony were German missionaries of the Rhenish Mission Society, who developed stations throughout the country. The missionaries managed to convert most of the Nama people, who had a strong cultural connection with the Calvinistic Dutch at the Cape. The Herero, however, were everywhere unwilling converts, being of proud African origins where tribal culture held firm and any avenue that led towards change was regarded with great suspicion. Nevertheless, the churches which those early missionaries built form the backbone of Christian faith in the country today.

The first European town established in Namibia was on the country's best-protected natural harbour. Here, a German trader, Adolf Lüderitz, opened a store in 1883, to serve the country's growing international trade, and the place later became known as Lüderitz Bay. Because internal strife among the indigenous people threatened to disrupt commerce, the Germans at Lüderitz Bay petitioned Prince Otto von Bismarck for protection. This was forthcoming and from here German authority moved quickly outwards, extending over the entire area of what is now Namibia within two years. Excluded was the coastal enclave from Sandwich Harbour to the Swakop River, which was retained by the British.

Under German protection, the country's white farming community grew in number, and expanded into the grazing lands traditionally held by the Hereros and Namas. Also, various taxes were introduced, and these factors caused growing dissent among the two black groups. Late in 1903, a Nama uprising drew most of the colonial *Schutztruppen* to the south. This gave Chief Kamaherero the chance that he had been waiting for and, in January 1904, widespread Herero rebellion broke out in the north. Numerous bloody battles followed, with the Hereros often supported by their

TOP *A number of tour and safari companies offer trips through the country's magnificent wild areas. Visitors can choose from a range including whistle-stop bus rides to see big game in the Etosha National Park, and four-wheel-drive excursions through the desert's awesome landscapes.*

CENTRE *Many of Namibia's mineral springs have been developed into resorts such as the one at Gross Barmen, with its indoor pool and private baths, as well as many outdoor attractions. Gross Barmen began as a Rhenish mission station in the mid-nineteenth century. Frequent plundering during the tribal wars of that time, however, led to its eventual abandonment.*

BOTTOM *The extraordinary baobab tree can be found in the northern areas of Namibia. The extremely thick trunks – large specimens can have boles with circumferences of up to 28 metres – have been known to be hollowed out and used as homes, prisons, storage barns, or even bush toilets.*

one-time foes, the Namas. Their efforts were in vain, however, and by the time peace was restored in 1905, the Hereros and Namas had lost up to 80 per cent of their people.

During the First World War, South Africa launched a naval and land assault on the country, forcing it to surrender, and at the Treaty of Versailles in 1919 the entire country was handed over to South Africa under the League of Nations' mandate system. The plan was to place former German colonies 'inhabited by peoples not yet able to stand by themselves' under protection of other, 'more advanced' countries.

In 1925, the small white population of the country was given limited powers of self-government. In 1948, the Nationalist Party came to power in South Africa, forcing its policies of racial segregation on Namibia. From about this time, decolonization of old European empires became an all-consuming trend across the globe. The United Nations put mounting pressure on South Africa to grant Namibia its independence, but time and again this was rejected as going against the spirit of its original mandate.

During the 1960s, the winds of *uhuru* (freedom) that were sweeping colonial Africa reached Namibia. From among the Ovambo people, who had succeeded the Herero and Nama as the country's dominant black group, the South West African People's Organization (Swapo) was formed. Within a short time Swapo's Marxist-aligned military wing instigated a guerrilla war against the occupying South African forces in Ovamboland. In 1975, civil war in Angola followed the hasty departure of the Portuguese. The South African army rushed in to support the anti-Marxist Unita army, while Cuban forces arrived to bolster the MPLA government there. The region's complex history of feuding seemed to be repeating itself.

With mounting international pressure and growing internal strife, an interim government was established in 1978, representing the country's non-Swapo aligned ethnic groups. This assembly survives today as the Democratic Turnhalle Alliance (DTA) – Swapo's main political rival.

In the same year, the United Nations Security Council approved Resolution 435, drawing up a blueprint for Namibian independence. However, South Africa argued that a full Cuban withdrawal from Angola was necessary before Namibia's independence could be considered. By early 1988, the opposing forces in Angola's civil war were held in a military deadlock; the time had finally come for pen to assert power. Since then, the world has witnessed the seemingly impossible achievement of Swapo and South Africa, Unita and the MPLA, Cuba, the Soviet Union and United States convening regularly to untangle the long history of political turmoil in the region. Finally, the floor was cleared for the country's first democratic elections, under the auspices of a United Nations task force and a special envoy of its Director-General.

With its rich diamond and uranium resources, its impressive wildlife reserves and vast conservation areas, a new independent Namibia promises to be an attractive country, both for foreign investors and for tourists who have delighted in the unique attractions of this country.

TOP *The fort of Namutoni was built for German colonial* Schutztruppen, *as a lonely outpost on the edge of swampy Ovamboland. It was raided and sacked by Ovambo forces, and later recaptured and rebuilt by the Germans. Today it serves as Etosha National Park's main rest camp. The fort houses a museum detailing its eventful history.*
CENTRE *The Ovambos, the country's largest ethnic group, are keen*

entrepreneurs. At Katima Mulilo, which until recently served as a military camp in Ovamboland, mobile hot-dog stalls and wood-carving displays satisfy tourists' needs.
BOTTOM *In the harsh Kaokoveld, a region of gnarled mountains and bleak desert plains, the Himba people live a meagre pastoral life that harks back to ancient times. The remote and aloof culture of the small Himba group, an*

offshoot of the Herero, has been largely bypassed by modernization.
OVERLEAF *Sunset reveals the stark outline of these tree aloes, in the so-called kokerboom forest near Keetmanshoop. The soft branches of these curious plants were hollowed out and used by San and Khoikhoi hunters as quivers for arrows, whence their common name (meaning 'quiver tree'), given by Dutch explorers from the Cape.*

TOP *Namaqua doves are common throughout Namibia's semi-desert and arid areas. They are usually seen singly or in pairs, except at water holes, where they congregate in large numbers.*

ABOVE *In the dry woodlands, scrubby hillsides and tree-lined watercourses of the arid west, fast-moving flocks of these attractive rosy-faced lovebirds can usually be taken as an indication of the direction to the nearest water source.*

LEFT *Over the millennia, as the continental surface has heaved and sagged, the Fish River has eroded the world's second deepest canyon into the sandstone bedrock.*

ABOVE *Wild horses of the Namib* Sperrgebiet *are the descendants of cavalry mounts let loose when the Germans surrendered to South African forces during the First World War. They are able to survive in this hostile, often waterless, environment, by virtue of a watering point made available by the mining company which controls the forbidden diamond area.*

LEFT *At a place called Mukurob, or the Finger of God, this sandstone formation gleams in the fading light of dusk. The actual 'finger' is now just rubble around its own base, having recently collapsed. The forces of erosion mostly go about their tasks in a slow, unnoticed manner. Occasionally, however, an event such as the Mukurob's demise will give us an explosive reminder of nature's ceaseless action.*

ABOVE *The Bogenfels rock arch is not often seen, for it lies on the country's forbidden diamond coast. The dolomite from which it is formed was created 600 million years ago on the bed of a primordial ocean, and the hungry sea is now reclaiming its own.*

LEFT *For an average of 50 days a year, thick fogs conceal the Skeleton Coast. Many boats and ships, mainly fishing trawlers, have run aground on this dreaded coastline and, once stranded, are 'captured' by the ever-shifting dunes.*

ABOVE *Gemsbok are superbly adapted to their desert environment: their shiny silver coats reflect sunlight; a network of vessels in their muzzles cools the blood, which reaches temperatures that would kill other mammals, before it arrives at the brain; and, most important, they can go for long periods without drinking, getting all their liquid requirements from the melons that grow in the desert's sands. Running in the still, midday heat, ironically enough, can help them to cool down.*

RIGHT *Few plants grow on the Namib desert's gravel plains, except the large camel thorn trees and tiny, usually overlooked lichens. The Namib is one of the world's major lichen belts: these plants, part fungus and part algae, are an important food source for some desert animals.*

OVERLEAF *A grey camel thorn tree stands defiantly, as though to halt the inevitable advance of these crescent-shaped sand dunes. The trees that one sees in the Namib grow along ill-defined watercourses, where they tap the regular subterranean flow.*

ABOVE *A side-winding Peringuey's adder is able to travel swiftly over the loose dune sands by using a longitudinal thrust motion, similar to that employed by sand-dwelling snakes throughout the world. Evolution has assisted this adder further, in that its scales resemble desert sand. It lies in ambush for its prey just under the dune's surface, only its raised eyes protruding.*

RIGHT *Wave upon wave of wind-driven sand dunes pulse across the Namib 'sand sea'. The serpentine crests of these dunes, near Sossusvlei, stand poised high above the ground, like liquid breakers frozen in motion.*

OVERLEAF *A lonely euphorbia succulent stands on the rough ground in the Namib-Naukluft Park. There are about 200 species of this distinctive genus in southern Africa. The plants have ill-formed flowers and few leaves, and the milky sap is used by indigenous people both as an arrow poison, and for medicinal and magical purposes.*

ABOVE *Rock monitors inhabit the semi-desert regions of Namibia. These primitive-looking creatures can reach lengths of well over a metre and, if threatened, may lash their tails and bite, holding on like a bulldog.*

LEFT *A most uncommon sight – flowing water in the Namib Desert. This stream in the Namib-Naukluft Park is the result of a cloudburst. The flow will soon cease, however, and dry earth will reign again.*

OVERLEAF *Greater flamingoes, the most attractive nomads of sub-Saharan Africa, feed in the few lagoons and shallow bays along the coast. They gather food by wading with their heavy beaks held upside down, filtering out small invertebrates and algae.*

ABOVE *The gnarled, twisted forms of camel thorn trees tell a tale of the savage harshness which must be endured for survival in the arid regions of Namibia.*

RIGHT *The kokerboom, which can reach a height of seven metres, is a conspicuous feature of the desert landscape, and frequently drew comment from early explorers.*

OVERLEAF *The Spitzkoppe was formed when a stream of molten minerals was forced up from the earth's core into the crust, beneath the surface. Here, it slowly cooled to form a rock mass. Horizontal erosion of the land has gradually revealed this huge plug of granite, where concentric exfoliation of the rock has given it its cone-like shape.*

LEFT *In a landscape so meagrely bestowed with plant life, each welwitschia plant becomes a semi-isolated ecosystem. An insect that depends entirely on this plant, and on which the plants depend for fertilization, is the welwitschia bug (Odontopus sexpunctatus). The yellow form is the adult bug, and the red form its larvae. The welwitschia is botanically fascinating in that it is an evolutionary link between cone-bearing and flowering plants.*

BELOW LEFT *Namibia's dry, rocky areas are the haunt of many types of geckos, skinks and agama lizards. The Brandberg mountain massif in particular is a haunt of rock-dwelling species such as this Agama planiceps.*

BELOW *Erosion caused by wind action and violent flash floods has gradually shaped many unusual rock formations throughout Namibia's arid regions. The Vingerklip ('finger rock') is a small remnant of a previous land surface near Xhorixas in Damaraland.*

TOP *The White Lady of the Brandberg is actually neither a lady nor European: the painting is of a young Negroid male, his body smeared white for ritual purposes.*

ABOVE *The engravings that can be viewed on the chunks of rock from fallen overhangs at Twyfelfontein are the finest examples of rock art to be found in southern Africa.*

LEFT *The inappropriately named Organ Pipes is one of the formations of the Burnt Mountain, near Xhorixas in Northern Damaraland.*

OVERLEAF *A black-backed jackal of the Skeleton Coast trots around a coastal lagoon, searching for carrion, birds' eggs or unguarded chicks.*

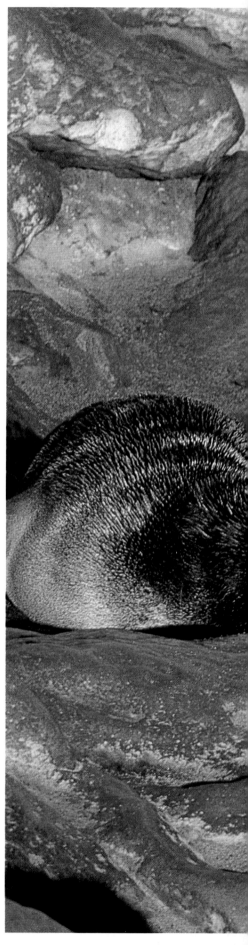

TOP *Nearly half the Namibian breeding population of jackass penguins is found on a handful of islands off the coast, although commercial overfishing and oil pollution have severely reduced their numbers. The penguins' common name comes from their loud braying call, usually issued at night or while they are out at sea in a fog.*

ABOVE *The sharp spines and sparse foliage deter browsing animals from this plant, but its single bloom attracts pollinators, thus allowing it to procreate.*

RIGHT *There are 24 breeding colonies of Cape fur seal off the southwest African coast. The males haul out in mid-October, when they fight to establish harems of breeding females. Servicing and protecting a harem is hard work and it continues throughout the mating period.*

ABOVE, ABOVE RIGHT and RIGHT *Namibia's coastline offers little hope to shipwrecked crews – trapped, as it is, between the icy Atlantic Ocean and the cruel Namib Desert. On the Skeleton Coast, the bleached remains of ships and seals, of whales and humans, lie scattered on the near-lifeless beaches. But the flotsam and jetsam from the sea brings relief to the beleaguered desert animals. When a dead whale washes up on a beach, it is not unusual to find lions feeding on the carcass. They will remain there, still feeding, long after the flesh has putrefied in the blistering sun.*

OVERLEAF *Legend tells us that twilight is the crack between night and day, when mysterious things are most likely to happen. This is the time of stealth, of the hunter and the hunted. As a herd of giraffes throws its silhouette against the backdrop of a fiery sunset, anticipation of the night hunt stirs excitement and fear.*

ABOVE *The ground squirrels that line the roadsides of the Etosha park, sitting on their haunches furiously nibbling seeds and grass stems, endear themselves to motorists. They often rush up to stationary vehicles with the acquired knowledge that these strange animals may offer food. But feeding wild animals is akin to issuing them with a death warrant, for then they come to rely on an artificial food source. When this food source runs out, they will die, in far greater numbers than would otherwise be the case.*

ABOVE LEFT *The leopard is seldom seen or heard, being such a solitary, secretive hunter of the night. But, in the Etosha National Park and other areas of the dry west where tree and hill cover is limited, leopards can sometimes be detected hunting in broad daylight.*

LEFT *The saddlebilled stork is one of the largest and most handsome wetland birds found in Namibia, standing approximately one and a half metres tall. The birds forage in shallow inland waters by walking slowly, or stirring up the mud, and jabbing at fish, frogs, molluscs and crustaceans, reptiles, birds and even small mammals.*

RIGHT *The Damara dik-dik is one of the smallest antelope found in southern Africa. It has a mobile nose that can be turned in any direction when sniffing for food. The pre-orbital scent glands, seen just below this dik-dik's eyes, secrete a fluid, used to mark each animal's territory. The name of this shy antelope comes from its behaviour when fleeing; with each bound it issues an explosive double whistle.*

BELOW *Despite the power and size of martial eagles, they are shy birds which avoid humans. They soar to great heights, and hunt by scanning the ground – either while gliding or from a perch. Their prey consists of game birds, waterfowl and owls, as well as large reptiles, and mammals such as goats, small antelope, hares and mongooses. They are common in most game reserves, but, like most other large raptors, are widely persecuted and poisoned by farmers.*

ABOVE *The nocturnal whitefaced owl eats mainly rodents, but is not averse to taking small birds such as this unfortunate redbilled quelea.*

LEFT *Little bee-eaters are found in open woodlands and along river banks. In Namibia, their range is confined to the small area of moist savanna found in the Caprivi Strip.*

FAR LEFT *An adult male elephant drinks as much as 100 litres of water a day to wash down the 200-odd kilograms of grass and leaves consumed in its 16 to 18 hours of feeding.*

63

ABOVE *Lionesses tend to be more proficient hunters than their mates, but whereas the females make the kills, the males claim the right of eating first.*

ABOVE RIGHT *Young male lions, like this one feeding on a fresh giraffe carcass, will be evicted from a pride once they come of breeding age. Male siblings will then form bachelor groups that hunt together: sometimes the groups will stay together even when the members have taken mates. The composition of prides can change considerably over the years, usually as a result of internal power struggles and the arrival of animals that have been rejected by other prides.*

RIGHT *Bat-eared foxes are the least aggressive of all carnivores – about 75 per cent of their diet consists of termites and beetle larvae, and, to a lesser extent, scorpions, small lizards, rodents and some wild fruit. They wander randomly around their territories, pointing their large ears to the ground. When they discern the sound of insect activity below the surface, they immediately begin to dig.*

ABOVE *Meyer's parrots are seldom easy to spot in the canopies of the tall trees they frequent in small groups. While foraging, the yellow shoulder flashes and high-pitched 'chee-chee', and dueted 'klink-kleep, chee-cheewee' calls are diagnostic. If disturbed, the group will drop out of the canopy and fly off in a fast-moving, low, direct line to the next perch.*

LEFT *By far the most numerous large mammals in Etosha National Park are the springbok – numbering about 26 000 at last count. These animals of the dry grasslands were once far more plentiful than they are today: early records tell of wagon trains having to stop for days to let huge herds of 'trekbokken' pass. Their migrations were finely attuned to following the rains across the arid regions, but fences and wanton hunting have all but put an end to these natural movements.*

ABOVE *The flightless ostrich is the largest of all living birds. Its diet consists mainly of insect and vegetable foodstuffs, and they will swallow small stones and pebbles to aid digestion. Food taken is collected in the gullet, and will eventually pass down the neck as a large ball, stretching the neck skin as it descends.*

LEFT *Herds of wildebeest and springbok graze the sweet grasses around the perimeter of the Etosha Pan – the place of dry water. Etosha was once part of a huge lake that covered most of northern Namibia, fed by numerous southward-flowing rivers. Then, the earth gave a mighty volcanic shrug and the south-flowing rivers were diverted to the west and east, developing new catchment areas, lakes and inland deltas, and leaving the old ones to slowly shrivel up.*

ABOVE *Black rhino are the most sought-after targets for Africa's increasingly sophisticated army of poachers. The horns of these animals are sold for exorbitantly high prices in North Yemen, where they are used to make traditional dagger handles, and in the Far East, where they are reputed to have aphrodisiacal properties. In fact, they are just hardened keratin, the same substance as hair. The Namibian conservation authorities have introduced a bold plan to save their few remaining rhinos – cutting off the horns.*

LEFT *Giraffes are the tallest animals on earth, the largest ones standing over five metres tall. To pump blood up to their lofty heads they also have the highest blood pressure of all animals. But for special valves in the neck arteries which regulate blood flow, their brains would burst when they lowered their heads to drink.*

OVERLEAF *The daily availability of drinking water is a prerequisite for the survival of the blue wildebeest. Because their natural migration routes have been cut off by man, Etosha's wildebeest rely on artificial water holes during the dry season.*

ABOVE *One of the more interesting species of Namibia's rich birdlife is the black korhaan: during courtship the male, seen here in repose, goes through a spectacular aerobatic sequence, rising into the air and then 'parachuting' slowly down to the accompaniment of a distinctively raucous call. The female is less of an exhibitionist and, while her mate performs, she remains hidden in the grass.*

ABOVE LEFT *The Kaokoveld is an uncompromising, rugged mountainland, with an only slightly higher rainfall than that of the Namib Desert. Yet people have made it their home. The Himba tribesmen of the area cling to the Kunene, the area's only perennial river. But, for grazing, they must move further into the wilderness, where a few permanent springs support them and their cattle.*

OVERLEAF *Two juvenile elephants of the arid Kaokoveld region huddle together during a sandstorm. Elephants are able to live in Namibia's semi-desert regions by virtue of the area's usually dry river beds. The wild fig, ebony, camel thorn and other large trees that grow along these watercourses provide a constant food supply in a land where grass is rare. Adult elephants teach the youngsters to dig into the river beds with their tusks until they strike the water table.*

ABOVE *Before disgorging its load into its land-locked delta in northwestern Botswana, the Okavango River passes over the Popa Rapids in Namibia's Caprivi strip.*

FAR LEFT *Dusk falls over the Okavango in the Caprivi Strip, always spectacular and primed with the intensity of the Bushveld wilderness.*

LEFT *Tree squirrels are confined to the savanna and subtropical forests of southern Africa; Etosha is the southwestern limit of their range. Watching them feeding and at play is fascinating, for they are most energetic and acrobatic creatures.*

The northeastern section of the country, bordering on Botswana, is called Bushmanland. It is the western fringe of the great Kalahari thirstland, which stretches from here, down through Botswana, to the western fringes of South Africa. The Kalahari is the last refuge of the San Bushmen, the Stone Age hunter-gatherers that once roamed all of southern Africa. With the coming of black and white farmers, they were hunted down and driven out of the more fertile areas. The survival of this Late Stone Age culture is a tenuous one, as more and more of these superb trackers and hunters are leaving the bush to settle around farms, army camps and government-provided waterholes. Here, as is the case with so many other ancient cultures, their social structures collapse and they succumb to the indignities of alcohol and prostitution.